Favourite Poems of England

Edited by
Jane McMorland Hunter

BATSFO

Dedication:

To Lily, with love.

First published in the United Kingdom in 2014.

This edition first published in the United Kingdom in 2017 by
Batsford
43 Great Ormond Street
London WC1N 3HZ

An imprint of Pavilion Books Company Ltd

ISBN: 9781849944595

A CIP catalogue record for this book is available from the
British Library.

23 22 21 20 19 18 17
10 9 8 7 6 5 4 3 2 1

Repro by Mission Productions, Hong Kong
Printed by 1010 Printing International Ltd, China

This book can be ordered direct from the publisher at the website:
www.pavilionbooks.com, or try your local bookshop.

Contents

Introduction

Great things are done when men and mountains meet.
(William Blake, *Gnomic Verses*)

Over the last thousand years the English landscape has totally changed, largely due to the hand of man. For better or worse, we have cleared forests, drained marshes, built cities and overlaid the countryside with a network of roads and railways. Most of the mountains and moors are now accessible and there is comparatively little left that is truly wild. While this is in some respects a disaster, there are advantages: many of our lives are easier, some of our cities are very beautiful and we can easily travel the length and breadth of the country and enjoy all that it has to offer.

This anthology is divided into ten sections, each looking at a different aspect of life in England. The first, This Sceptred Isle, takes a somewhat idyllic look at the country as a whole and offers a brief history, courtesy of Rudyard Kipling and an anonymous rhyme about the kings and queens. Camelot no longer exists and it would be stretching the imagination to describe much of the country as a 'demi-paradise', but there is nothing to stop us dreaming. The poems then travel round the country, from Tennyson's house in Sussex, to Norman Nicholson's wall traversing the fells. Emily Brontë finds true wildness, but further south Romney Marsh is seen as 'ripe for development' in U. A. Fanthorpe's poem. Lords and Ladies all Assembled is not just about the nobility, but also includes a foddering boy, a nun, a Roman centurion and, perhaps our best-known king, Henry VIII.

City life and rural life divide the country with 'the million-peopled lanes and alleys' contrasting with a 'lark's early carrols' saluting the new day. London, Oxford, Cambridge and Bath contrast with the anonymous cities of H. D., while rural life revolves around haymaking, meadows and a rather unprincipled vicar. Wherever it may be, an Englishman's home is his castle. The poems here range from grand country estates to charming cottages. Beautiful old mansions may house misers, while modern villas can be homes to writers and musicians. The varieties are endless but, in an ideal world, all are surrounded by a garden with 'a thousand beauties' and in possession of a 'stately view'.

As important as our work is our leisure – we all need time to stand and stare or play. Football, cricket, tennis and fishing have inspired poets down the ages, but so too have floating down a river, walking on a beach or suffering the trials and tribulations of a pony that has swallowed its bit. Nearly all these activities are better when accompanied by sandwiches and a flask of something hot.

One of the things we have little control over is the weather. Each season brings forth a new set of experiences and occasional delights. Even if our seasons don't always arrive on time, they do at least provide moments of great beauty and surprise – 'the flame-red harvest moon' or droplets of water shining 'like silver buttons' in a fog. The penultimate section includes some of the things that are unusual to England: St. George and his dragon, morris dancers and the mysteries of Stonehenge. Corner shops, wiggly roads and museums that open sporadically can all be found in other countries but, equally, can have something uniquely English about them.

The final section is largely written by poets who are away from England. Absence makes the heart grow fonder and this is particularly true of these poems. For those abroad it is easy to focus on England's charms, travel at home often inspires more cynicism, as we can see in Byron's *Don Juan*.

Apart from one or two snipes about the climate, the class system and the roads, the majority of poems have been chosen to show the charming and attractive face of England – faults it may have, but there is also much that is good. England has inspired many poets to write at length and, unfortunately, some of the poems had to be cut. In these cases I have chosen extracts that I feel describe a particular feature of England and hope that they will inspire the reader to search out the poem in its entirety. Where possible, I have chosen the version that is closest to that which the poet originally wrote; this may lead to some unusual spellings and unfamiliar words but if they make the reader pause and think, so much the better.

This Sceptred Isle

The Kings and Queens
of England

Willy, Willy, Harry, Ste,
Harry, Dick, John, Harry three.
Edwards one, two three, then who?
The weak and wicked Richard two.

Henrys four, five six and then
Edwards four, five and Dick again.
Henrys seven and eight, six wives no less,
Then Edward, Mary and Good Queen Bess.

Next James and Charles the Stuarts came,
Then Oliver Cromwell, Protector by name,
Charles two, James two, then the double plan,
With William and Mary and lastly Queen Anne.

Hanover Georges one, two, three and four,
A fourth William and Victoria for years sixty-four.
Edward the seventh and then George five,
Edward eight, George six and our Queen, still alive.

Anon

This Royal Throne of Kings

from: Richard II, Act II scene i

This royal throne of kings, this sceptred isle,
This earth of majesty, this seat of Mars,
This other Eden, demi-paradise,
This fortress built by Nature for herself
Against infection and the hand of war,
This happy breed of men, this little world,
This precious stone set in the silver sea,
Which serves it in the office of a wall,
Or as a moat defensive to a house,
Against the envy of less happier lands,
This blessèd plot, this earth, this realm, this England.

William Shakespeare
(1564–1616)

Sonnet

Happy is England! I could be content
    To see no other verdure than its own;
    To feel no other breezes than are blown
Through its tall woods with high romances blent:
Yet do I sometimes feel a languishment
    For skies Italian, and an inward groan
    To sit upon an Alp as on a throne,
And half forget what world or worldling meant.
Happy is England, sweet her artless daughters;
    Enough their simple loveliness for me,
        Enough their whitest arms in silence clinging:
    Yet do I often warmly burn to see
        Beauties of deeper glance, and hear their singing,
And float with them about the summer waters.

John Keats
(1795–1821)

By Severn

If England, her spirit lives anywhere
It is by Severn, by hawthorns and grand willows.
Earth heaves up twice a hundred feet in air
And ruddy clay-falls scooped out to the weedy shallows.
There in the brakes of May Spring has her chambers,
Robing-rooms of hawthorn, cowslip, cuckoo flower –
Wonder complete changes for each square joy's hour,
Past thought miracles are there and beyond numbers.
If for the drab atmospheres and managed lighting
In London town, Oriana's playwrights had
Wainlode her theatre and then coppice-clad
Hill for her ground of sauntering and idle waiting,
Why, then I think, our chiefest glory of pride
(The Elizabethans of Thames, South and Northern side)
Would nothing of its meeding be denied,
And her sons praises from England's mouth again be outcried.

Ivor Gurney
(1890–1937)

England I Love Thee

from: Beppo, verses XLVII–XLVIX

'England! with all thy faults I love thee still',
    I said at Calais, and have not forgot it;
I like to speak and lucubrate my fill;
    I like the government (but that is not it);
I like the freedom of the press and quill;
    I like the Habeas Corpus (when we've got it);
I like a Parliamentary debate,
Particularly when 'tis not too late;

I like the taxes, when they're not too many;
    I like a seacoal fire, when not too dear;
I like a beef-steak, too, as well as any;
    Have no objection to a pot of beer;
I like the weather, – when it is not rainy,
    That is, I like two months of every year.
And so God save the Regent, Church, and King!
Which means that I like all and everything.

Our standing army, and disbanded seamen,
    Poor's rate, Reform, my own, the nation's debt,
Our little riots just to show we are free men,
    Our trifling bankruptcies in the Gazette,
Our cloudy climate, and our chilly women,
    All these I can forgive, and those forget,
And greatly venerate our recent glories,
And wish they were not owing to the Tories.

George Gordon, Lord Byron
(1788–1824)

Puck's Song

Enlarged from Puck of Pook's Hill

See you in the ferny ride that steals
Into the oak-woods far?
O that was whence they hewed the keels
That rolled to Trafalgar.

And mark you where the ivy clings
To Bayham's mouldering walls?
O there we cast the stout railings
That stand around St. Paul's.

See you the dimpled track that runs
All hollow through the wheat?
O that was where they hauled the guns
That smote King Philip's fleet.

Out of the Weald, the secret Weald,
Men sent in ancient years
The horse-shoes red at Flodden Field,
The arrows at Poitiers!

See you our little mill that clacks,
So busy by the brook?
She has ground her corn and paid her tax
Ever since Doomesday Book.

See you our stilly woods of oak,
And the dread ditch beside?
O that was where the Saxons broke
On the day that Harold died.

See you the windy levels spread
About the gates of Rye?
O that was where the Northmen fled,
When Alfred's ships came by.

See you our pastures wide and lone,
Where the red oxen browse?
O there was a City thronged and known,
Ere London boasted a house.

And see you, after rain, the trace
Of mound and ditch and wall?
O that was a Legion's camping-place,
When Caesar sailed from Gaul.

And see you the marks that show and fade,
Like shadows on the Downs?
O they are the lines the Flint Men made,
To guard their wondrous towns.

Trackway and Camp and City lost,
Salt Marsh where now is corn –
Old Wars, old Peace, old Arts that cease,
And so was England born!

She is not any common Earth,
Water or wood or air,
But Merlin's Isle of Gramarye,
Where you and I will fare!

Rudyard Kipling
(1865–1936)

The Lady of Shalott

Part I

On either side the river lie
Long fields of barley and of rye,
That clothe the wold and meet the sky;
And thro' the field the road runs by
    To many-tower'd Camelot;
And up and down the people go,
Gazing where the lilies blow
Round an island there below,
    The island of Shalott.

Willows whiten, aspens quiver,
Little breezes dusk and shiver
Thro' the wave that runs for ever
By the island in the river
    Flowing down to Camelot.
Four grey walls and four grey towers,
Overlook a space of flowers,
And the silent isle imbowers
    The Lady of Shalott.

By the margin, willow-veil'd,
Slide the heavy barges trail'd
By slow horses; and unhail'd
The shallop flitteth silken-sail'd
    Skimming down to Camelot:
But who hath seen her wave her hand?
Or at the casement seen her stand?
Or is she known in all the land,
    The Lady of Shalott?

Only reapers, reaping early
In among the bearded barley,
Hear a song that echoes cheerly
From the river winding clearly,
　　Down to tower'd Camelot:
And by the moon the reaper weary,
Piling sheaves in uplands airy,
Listening, whispers ''Tis the fairy
　　Lady of Shalott.'

Alfred, Lord Tennyson
(1809–1892)

The Map

How tiny England is this map will show,
And how she is the butt of many seas
That shaped her landscape to its subtleties,
How few her rivers are, her hills how low.
This map will tell you, faintly, of her towns
Pin-point for London, Thames a thread of hair
But will not tell of dewponds on the Downs,
Or how the leaves of Warwick green the air.
This map will tell you nothing of the way
The coltish April skips across her skies.
Nor how, in autumn nights, the curlew cries,
Or thrush or blackbird harmonize in May...
For these such things consult that wiser chart
Engraved upon the exiled English heart.

James Walker
(1911–1982)

Properte of
Every Shire

The Properties of the Shires of England

The properte of every shire
I shall you tell, and ye will hear.
Herefordshire shield and spear;
Worsetshire wring pear.
Gloucetershire shoe and nail;
Bristowe ship and sail.
Oxenfordshire gird the mare:
Warwykshire bind bere.
London restore:
Sowtherey great bragere.
Esex full of good hoswifes:
Middlesex full of strives.
Kentshire hot as fire:
Sowseke full of dirt and mire.
Hertfordshire full of wood:
Huntingdonshire corn full good.
Bedfordshire is nought to lack:
Bokinghamshire is his make.
Northamptonshire full of love
Beneath the girdle and not above.
Lancastreshire fair archere:
Chestreshire thwakkere.
Northumbreland hasty and hot:
Westmorland tot for sote!
Yorkshire full of knights:

Lincolnshire men full of mightes.
Cambridgeshire full of pikes:
Holand full of great dykes.
Norfolk full of wiles:
Southfolk full of stiles.
I am of *Shropshire* my shins be sharp:
Lay wood to the fyre, and dresse me my harpe.
Notinghamshire full of hogs:
Derbyshire full of dogs.
Leicetershire full of beans:
Staffordshire full of queans.
Wiltshire fair and plain:
Barkshire fill the wain.
Hampshire dry and wete.
Somersetshire good for wheat.
Devenshire mighty and strong:
Dorsetshire will have no wrong.
Pinnokshire is not to praise:
A man may go it in two days.
Cornewaile full of tin:
Walis full of goote and kene.
That Lord that for us all did die
Save all these shires. *Amen* say I.

Anon

Aldworth House, Black Down

from: Prologue to General Hamley,
The Charge of the Heavy Brigade at Balaclava

Our birches yellowing and from each
    The light leaf falling fast,
While squirrels from our fiery beech
    Were bearing off the mast,
You came, and look'd and loved the view
    Long-known and loved by me,
Green Sussex fading into blue
    With one gray glimpse of sea.

Alfred, Lord Tennyson
(1809–1892)

*In 1867 Alfred, Lord Tennyson bought 60 acres on Black Down, the
highest point on the North Downs. There he built a house as a retreat
from the summer crowds. The view looked out over the Sussex Weald
and the English Channel, forty miles away.*

The North Country

In another country, black poplars shake themselves over a pond,
And rooks and the rising smoke-waves scatter and wheel from the
    works beyond:
The air is dark with north and with sulphur, the grass is a darker
    green,
And people darkly invested with purple move palpable through the
    scene.

Soundlessly down across the counties, out of the resonant gloom
That wraps the north in stupor and purple travels the deep, slow
    boom
Of the man-life north- imprisoned, shut in the hum of the purpled
    steel
As it spins to sleep on its motion, drugged dense in the sleep of the
    wheel.

Out of the sleep, from the gloom of motion, soundlessly,
    somnambule
Moans and booms the soul of a people imprisoned, asleep in the rule
Of the strong machine that runs mesmeric, booming the spell of its
    word
Upon them and moving them helpless, mechanic, their will to its
    will deferred.

Yet all the while comes the droning inaudible, out of the violet air,
The moaning of sleep-bound beings in travail that toil and are will-
    less there
In the spellbound north, convulsive now with a dream near morning,
    strong
With violent achings heaving to burst the sleep that is now not long.

D. H. Lawrence
(1885–1930)

High Waving Heather

High waving heather 'neath stormy blasts bending,
Midnight and moonlight and bright shining stars,
Darkness and glory rejoicingly blending,
Earth rising to heaven and heaven descending,
Man's spirit away from its drear dongeon sending,
Bursting the fetters and breaking the bars.

All down the mountain sides wild forests lending,
One mighty voice to the life-giving wind,
Rivers their banks in the jubilee rending,
Fast through the valleys a reckless course wending,
Wider and deeper their waters extending,
Leaving a desolate desert behind.

Shining and lowering and swelling and dying,
Charging forever from midnight to noon,
Roaring like thunder like soft music sighing,
Shadows on shadows advancing and flying,
Lightning bright flashes the deep gloom defying,
Coming as swiftly and fading as soon.

Emily Brontë
(1818–1848)

Cambridgeshire

The stacks, like blunt impassive temples, rise
Across flat fields against autumnal skies.
The hairy-footed horses plough the land,
Or as in prayer and meditation stand
Upholding square, primeval, dung-stained carts,
With an unending patience in their hearts.

Nothing is changed. The farmer's gig goes by
Against the horizon. Surely, the same sky,
So vast and yet familiar, grey and mild,
And streaked with light like music, I, a child,
Lifted my face from leaf-edged lanes to see,
Late-coming home, to bread-and-butter tea.

Frances Cornford
(1886–1960)

The Song of the Western Men

A good sword and a trusty hand!
    A merry heart and true!
King James's men shall understand
    What Cornish lads can do!

And have they fixed the where and when?
    And shall Trelawney die?
Here's twenty thousand Cornish men
    Will know the reason why!

Out spake their Captain brave and bold:
    A merry wight was he:–
'If London Tower were Michael's hold,
    We'd set Trelawney free!

'We'll cross the Tamar, land to land:
    The Severn is no stay:
With "one and all," and hand in hand:
    And who shall bid us nay?

'And when we come to London Wall,
    A pleasant sight to view,
Come forth! come forth! ye cowards all:
    Here's men as good as you.

'Trelawney he's in keep and hold:
    Trelawney he may die:
But here's twenty thousand Cornish bold
    Will know the reason why!'

Rev. Robert Stephen Hawker
(1803-1875)

Wall

The wall walks the fell –
Grey millipede on slow
Stone hooves;
Its slack back hollowed
At gulleys and grooves,
Or shouldering over
Old boulders
Too big to be rolled away.
Fallen fragments
Of the high crags
Crawl in the walk of the wall.

A dry-stone wall
Is a wall and a wall,
Leaning together
(Cumberland-and-Westmorland
Champion wrestlers),
Greening and weathering,
Flank by flank,
With filling of rubble
Between the two –
A double-rank
Stone dyke:
Flags and through –
stones jutting out sideways,
Like the steps of a stile.

A wall walks slowly.
At each give of the ground,
Each creak of the rock's ribs,
It puts its foot gingerly,
Arches its hogs-holes,
Lets cobble and knee-joint
Settle and grip.
As the slipping fellside
Erodes and drifts,
The wall shifts with it,
Is always on the move.

They built a wall slowly,
A day a week;
Built it to stand,
But not stand still.
They built a wall to walk.

Norman Nicholson
(1914–1987)

Adlestrop

Yes. I remember Adlestrop –
The name, because one afternoon
Of heat the express-train drew up there
Unwontedly. It was late June.

The steam hissed. Someone cleared his throat.
No one left and no one came
On the bare platform. What I saw
Was Adlestrop – only the name

And willows, willow-herb, and grass,
And meadowsweet, and haycocks dry,
No whit less still and lonely fair
Than the high cloudlets in the sky.

And for that minute a blackbird sang
Close by, and round him, mistier,
Farther and farther, all the birds
Of Oxfordshire and Gloucestershire.

Edward Thomas
(1878–1917)

A Major Road for Romney Marsh

It is a kingdom, a continent.
Nowhere is like it.
           (Ripe for development)

It is salt, solitude, strangeness.
It is ditches, and windcurled sheep.
It is sky over sky after sky.
           (It wants hard shoulders, Happy Eaters,
           Heavy breathing of HGVs)

It is obstinate hermit trees.
It is small truculent churches
Huddling under the gale force.
           (It wants WCs, Kwiksaves,
           Artics, Ind Ests, Jnctns)

It is the Military Canal
Minding its peaceable business
Between the Levels and the Marsh.
           (It wants *investing in roads,*
           Sgns syng T'DEN, F'STONE, C'BURY)

It is itself, and different.
           (Nt fr lng. Nt fr lng.)

U. A. Fanthorpe
(1929–2009)

Lords and Ladies all Assembled

The Garden Party

The Rich arrived in pairs
And also in Rolls Royces;
They talked of their affairs
In loud and strident voices.

(The Husbands and the Wives
Of this select society
Lead independent lives
Of infinite variety.)

The Poor arrived in Fords,
Whose features they resembled;
They laughed to see so many Lords
And Ladies all assembled.

The People in Between
Looked underdone and harassed
And out of place and mean,
And horribly embarrassed.

For the hoary social curse
Gets hoarier and hoarier,
And it stinks a trifle worse
Than in the days of Queen Victoria,
When they married and gave in marriage,
They danced at the County Ball,
And some of them kept a carriage,
And the flood destroyed them all.

Hilaire Belloc
(1870–1953)

Good English Hospitality

from: Songs from an Island in the Moon

This city and this country has brought forth many mayors
To sit in state, and give forth laws out of their old oak chairs,
With face as brown as any nut with drinking of strong ale –
Good English hospitality, O then it did not fail!

With scarlet gowns and broad gold lace, would make a yeoman
    sweat;
With stockings roll'd above their knees and shoes as black as jet;
With eating beef and drinking beer, O they were stout and hale –
Good English hospitality, O then it did not fail!

Thus sitting at a table wide the mayor and aldermen
Were fit to give law to the city; each ate as much as ten:
The hungry poor enter'd the hall to eat good beef and ale –
Good English hospitality, O then it did not fail!

William Blake
(1757–1827)

The Nun

from: The Canterbury Tales: The Prologue

Ther was also a Nonne, a prioresse,
That of hir smyling was ful simple and coy;
Hir gretteste ooth was but by sëynt Loy;
And she was cleped madame Eglentyne.
Ful wel she song the service divyne,
Entuned in hir nose ful semely;
And Frensh she spake ful faire and fetisly,
After the scole of Stratford atte Bowe,
For Frensh of Paris was to hir unknowe.
At mete wel y-taught was she with-alle;
She leet no morsel from hir lippes falle,
Ne wette hir fingers in hir sauce depe,
Wel coude she carie a morsel, and wel kepe,
That no drop ne fille up-on hir brest,
In curteisye was set ful muchel hir lest.
Hir over-lippe wiped she so clene,
That in hir coppe was no ferthyng sene
Of grece, when she dronken hadde hir draughte.
Ful semely after hir mete she raughte,
And sikerley she was of greet disport,
And ful plesaunt, and amyable of port,
And peyned hir to countrefete cheere
Of court, and been estatlich of manere,
And to ben holden digne of reverence.

Geoffrey Chaucer
(c1340–1400)

The Foddering Boy

The foddering boy along the crumping snows
With straw-band-belted legs and folded arm
Hastens and on the blast that keenly blows
Oft turns for breath and beats his fingers warm
And shakes the lodging snow from off his clothes,
Buttoning his doublet closer from the storm
And slouching his brown beaver o'er his nose,
Then faces it again – and sees the stack
Within its circling fence – where hungry lows
Expecting cattle making many a track
About the snows – impatient for the sound
When in huge fork-fulls trailing at his back
He litters the sweet hay about the ground
And brawls to call the staring cattle round.

John Clare
(1793–1864)

Henry VIII

Bluff King Hal was full of beans;
He married half a dozen queens;
For three called Kate they cried the banns,
And one called Jane, and a couple of Annes.

The first he asked to share his reign
Was Kate of Aragon, straight from Spain –
But when his love for her was spent,
He got a divorce, and out she went.

Anne Boleyn was his second wife;
He swore to cherish her all his life –
But seeing a third he wished instead,
He chopped off poor Anne Boleyn's head.

He married the next afternoon
Jane Seymour, which was rather soon –
But one year after as his bride
She crept into her bed and died.

Anne of Cleves was Number Four;
Her portrait thrilled him to the core –
But when he met her face to face
Another royal divorce took place.

Catherine Howard, Number Five,
Billed and cooed to keep alive –
But one day Henry felt depressed;
The executioner did the rest.

Sixth and last was Catherine Parr,
Sixth and last and luckiest far –
For this time it was Henry who
Hopped the twig, and a good job too.

Eleanor and Herbert Farjeon
(1881–1965, 1887–1945)

The Roman Centurion's Song

(Roman occupation of Britain, A. D. 300)

Legate, I had the news last night – my cohort ordered home
By ship to Portus Itius and thence by road to Rome.
I've marched the companies aboad, the arms are stowed below:
Now let another take my sword. Command me not to go!

I've served in Britain forty years, from Vectis to the Wall.
I have none other home than this, nor any life at all.
Last night I did not understand, but, now the hour draws near
That calls me to my native land, I feel that land is here.

Here where men say my name was made, here where my work was
    done;
Here where my dearest dead are laid – my wife – my wife and son;
Here where time, custom, grief, and toil, age, memory, service, love,
Have rooted me in British soil. Ah, how can I remove?

For me this land, that sea, these airs, those folk and fields suffice.
What purple Southern pomp can match our changeful Northern
    skies,
Black with December snows unshed or pearled with August haze –
The clanging arch of steel-grey March, or June's long-lighted days?

You'll follow widening Rhodanus till vine and olive lean
Aslant before the sunny breeze that sweeps Nemausus clean
To Arelate's triple gate; but let me linger on,
Here where our stiff-necked British oaks confront Euroclydon!

You'll take the old Aurelian Road through shore-descending pines
Where, blue as any peacock's neck, the Tyrrhene Ocean shines.
You'll go where laurel crowns are won, but – will you e'er forget
The scent of hawthorn in the sun, or bracken in the wet?

Let me work here for Britain's sake – at any task you will –
A marsh to drain, a road to make or native troops to drill.
Some Western camp (I know the Pict) or granite Border keep,
Mid seas of heather derelict, where our old messmates sleep.

Legate, I come to you in tears – My cohort ordered home!
I've served in Britain forty years. What should I do in Rome?
Here is my heart, my soul, my mind – the only life I know.
I cannot leave it all behind. Command me not to go!

Rudyard Kipling
(1865–1936)

Italian Opera

In Days of Old, when *Englishmen* were – *Men,*
Their Musick, like themselves, was grave and plain;
The manly Trumpet, the simple Reed,
Alike with *Citizen* and *Swain* agreed;
Whose Songs, in lofty Sense, but humble Verse,
Their Loves and Wars alternately rehearse;
Sung by themselves, their homely Cheer to crown,
In Tunes from Sire to Son deliver'd down.

But now, since *Britains* are become polite,
Since Few can *read,* and Fewer still can *write;*
Since Trav'ling has so much improv'd our *Beaux,*
That each brings home a foreign *Tongue,* or – *Nose;*
And Ladies paint with that amazing Grace,
That their best *Vizard* is their natural *Face;*
Since *South-Sea Schemes* have so inrich'd the Land,
That *Footmen* 'gainst their *Lords* for *Boroughs* stand;
Since *Masquerades* and *Op'ras* made their Entry,
And *Heydegger* reign'd *Guardian* of our Gentry;
A hundred various Instruments combine,
And foreign *Songsters* in the Concert join:
The *Gallick Horn,* those winding Tube in vain
Pretends to emulate the *Trumpet's* Strain;
The *shrill-ton'd Fiddle,* and the *warbling Flute,*

The *grave Bassoon, deep Base*, and *tinkling Lute*,
The *jingling Spinnet*, and the *full-mouth'd Drum*,
A *Roman Capon*, and *Venetian Strum*,
All league, melodious Nonsense to dispense,
And give us *Sound*, and *Show*, instead of *Sense*;
In unknown Tongues mysterious Dullness chant,
Make Love in Tune, or thro' the Gamut rant.

James Miller
(1703–1744)

The Parks, the Squares, the Thoroughfares

The Two Loves

I have two loves, and one is dark,
    The other fair as may be seen;
My dark love is Old London Town,
    My fair love is the Country green.

My fair love has a sweeter breath,
    A clearer face by day; and nights
So wild with stars that dazzled I
    See multitudes of *other* lights.

My dark love has her domes, as round
    As mushrooms in my fair love's meadows:
While both my loves have houses old,
    Whose windows look cross-eyed at shadows.

W. H. Davies
(1871–1940)

London

Athwart the sky a lowly sigh
    From west to east the sweet wind carried;
The sun stood still on Primrose Hill;
    His light in all the city tarried:
The clouds on viewless columns bloomed
Like smouldering lilies unconsumed.

'Oh sweetheart, see! how shadowy,
    Of some occult magician's rearing,
Or swung in space of heaven's grace
    Dissolving, dimly reappearing,
Afloat upon ethereal tides
St. Paul's above the city rides!'

A rumour broke through the thin smoke
    Enwreathing abbey, tower, and palace,
The parks, the squares, the thoroughfares,
    The million-peopled lanes and alleys,
An ever-muttering prisoned storm,
The heart of London beating warm.

John Davidson
(1857–1909)

The Great Frost

from: Trivia or the Art of Walking the Streets of London

O roving Muse, recal that wond'rous Year,
When winter reign'd in bleak *Britannia's* Air;
When hoary *Thames,* with frosted Osiers crown'd
Was three long Moons in icy Fetters bound.
The Waterman, forlorn along the Shore,
Pensive reclines upon his useless Oar,
Sees harness'd Steeds desert the stony Town,
And wander Roads unstable, not their own:
Wheels o'er the harden'd Waters smoothly glide,
And rase with whiten'd Tracks the slipp'ry Tide.
Here the fat Cook piles high the blazing Fire,
And scarce the Spit can turn the Steer entire.
Booths sudden hide the *Thames,* long Streets appear,
And num'rous Games proclaim the crouded Fair.
So when a General bids the martial Train
Spread their Encampment o'er the spacious Plain;
Thick-rising Tents a Canvas City build,
And the loud Dice resound thro' all the Field.

John Gay
(1685–1732)

Street after Street

from: Cities

Can we believe – by an effort
comfort our hearts:
it is not waste all this,
not placed here in disgust,
street after street,
each patterned alike,
no grace to lighten
a single house of the hundred
crowded into one garden-space.

Crowded – can we believe,
not in utter disgust,
in ironical play –
but the maker of cities grew faint
with the beauty of temple
and space before temple,
arch upon perfect arch,
of pillars and corridors that led out
to strange court-yards and porches
where sun-light stamped
hyacinth-shadows
black on pavement.

That the maker of cities grew faint
with the splendour of palaces,
paused while the incense-flowers
from the incense-trees
dropped on the marble-walk,

thought anew; fashioned this –
street after street alike.

For alas,
he had crowded the city so full
that men could not grasp beauty,
beauty was over them,
through them, about them,
no crevice unpacked with the honey,
rare, measureless.

So he built a new city,
ah can we believe, not ironically
but for new splendour
constructed new people
to lift through slow growth
to a beauty unrivalled yet –
and created new cells,
hideous first, hideous now –
spread larve across them,
not honey but seething life.

And in those dark cells,
packed street after street,
souls live, hideous yet –
O disfigured, defaced,
with no trace of the beauty
men once held so light.

H. D. (Hilda Dolittle)
(1886–1961)

The Lamplighter

When the light of day declineth,
And a swift angel through the sky
Kindleth God's tapers clear,
With ashen staff the lamplighter
Passeth along the darkling streets
To light our earthly lamps;

Lest, prowling in the darkness,
The thief should haunt with quiet tread,
Or men on evil errands set;
Or wayfarers be benighted;
Or neighbours, bent from house to house,
Should need a guiding torch.

He is like a needlewoman
Who deftly on a sable hem
Stitches in gleaming jewels;
Or, haply, he is like a hero,
Whose bright deeds on the long journey
Are beacons on our way.

And when in the East cometh morning,
And the broad splendour of the sun,
Then, with the tune of little birds
Ringing on high, the lamplighter
Passeth by each quiet house,
And putteth out the lamps.

Walter de la Mare
(1873–1956)

Oxford

from: The Triumph of Isis

Ye venerable bow'rs, ye seats sublime,
Clad in the mossy vest of fleeting time;
Ye stately piles of old munificence,
At once the pride of Learning and defence;
Where ancient Piety, a matron hoar,
Still seems to keep the hospitable door;
Ye cloisters pale, that, length'ning to the sight,
Still step by step to musings mild invite;
Ye high-arched walks, where oft the bard has caught
The glowing sentiment, the lofty thought;
Ye temples dim, where pious duty pays
Her holy hymns of ever-echoing praise; –
Lo! your lov'd Isis, from the bord'ring vale,
With all a mother's fondness, bids you hail! –
Hail, Oxford, hail! of all that's good and great,
Of all that's fair, the guardian and the seat;
Nurse of each brave pursuit, each generous aim,
By truth exalted to the throne of fame!

Thomas Warton
(1728–1790)

Residence at Cambridge

from: The Prelude

It was a dreary morning when the wheels
Rolled over a wide plain o'erhung with clouds,
And nothing cheered our way till first we saw
The long-roofed chapel of King's College lift
Turrets and pinnacles in answering files,
Extended high above a dusky grove.

Advancing, we espied upon the road
A student clothed in gown and tasselled cap,
Striding along as if o'ertasked by Time,
Or covetous of exercise and air;
He passed – nor was I master of my eyes
Till he was left an arrow's flight behind.
As near and nearer to the spot we drew,
It seemed to suck us in with an eddy's force.
Onward we drove beneath the Castle; caught,
While crossing Magdalene Bridge, a glimpse of Cam;
And at the *Hoop* alighted, famous Inn.

My spirit was up, my thoughts were full of hope;
Some friends I had, acquaintances who there
Seemed friends, poor simple schoolboys, now hung round
With honour and importance: in a world
Of welcome faces up and down I roved;
Questions, directions, warnings and advice,
Flowed in upon me, from all sides; fresh day
Of pride and pleasure! to myself I seemed
A man of business and expense, and went

From shop to shop about my own affairs,
To Tutor or to Tailor, as befell,
From street to street with loose and careless mind.

    I was the Dreamer, they the Dream; I roamed
Delighted through the motley spectacle;
Gowns grave or gaudy, doctors, students, streets,
Courts, cloisters, flocks of churches, gateways, towers:
Migration strange for a stripling of the hills,
A northern villager.

William Wordworth
(1770–1850)

Letter from Bath

from: Letter VII

Of all the gay Places the World can afford,
By Gentle and Simple for Pastime ador'd,
Fine Balls, and fine Concerts, fine Buildings, and Springs,
Fine Walks, and fine Views, and a thousand fine Things,
Not to mention the sweet Situation and Air,
What Place, my dear Mother, with *Bath* can compare?
Let *Bristol* for Commerce and Dirt be renown'd,
At *Sal'sbury* Pen Knives and Scissars be ground;
The Towns of *Devizes*, of *Bradford*, and *Frome*,
May boast that they better can manage the Loom;
I believe that they may;– but the World to refine,
In Manners, in Dress, in Politeness to shine,
O *Bath*! let the Art, let the Glory be thine.

Christopher Anstey
(1724–1805)

In a Cathedral City

These people have not heard your name;
No loungers in this placid place
Have helped to bruit your beauty's fame.

The grey Cathedral, towards whose face
Bend eyes untold, has met not yours;
Your shade has never swept its base,

Your form has never darkened its doors,
Nor have your faultless feet once thrown
A pensive pit-pat on its floors.

Along the street to maids well known
Blithe lovers hum their tender airs
but in your praise voice not a tone....

– Since nought bespeaks you here, or bears,
As I, your imprint through and through,
Here might I rest, till my heart shares
The spot's unconsciousness of you!
Salisbury

Thomas Hardy
(1840–1928)

Haymakers Resting in the Sun

Evenen in the Village

Now the light o' the west is a-turn'd to gloom,
  An' the men be at hwome vrom ground;
An' the bells be a-zendèn all down the Coombe
  From tower, their mwoansome sound.
        An' the wind is still,
      An' the house-dogs do bark,
An' the rooks be a-vled to the elems high an' dark,
    An' the water do roar at mill.

An' the flickerén light drough the window-peäne
  Vrom the candle's dull fleäme do shoot,
An' young Jemmy the smith is a-gone down leäne,
  A-pläyén his shrill-vaïced flute.
        An' the miller's man
      Do zit down at his ease
On the seat that is under the cluster o' trees,
    Wi' his pipe an' his cider can.

William Barnes
(1801–1886)

Harvest Hymn

We spray the fields and scatter
    The poison on the ground
So that no wicked wild flowers
    Upon our farm be found.
We like whatever helps us
    To line our purse with pence;
The twenty-four hour broiler house
    And neat electric fence.

All concrete sheds around us
    And Jaguars in the yard,
The telly lounge and deep-freeze
    Are ours from working hard.

We fire the fields for harvest,
    The hedges swell the flame,
The oak trees and the cottages
    From which our fathers came.
We give no compensation,
    The earth is ours today,
And if we lose on arable,
    The bungalows will pay.

All concrete sheds... etc.

John Betjeman
(1906–1984)

The Miller

In a plain pleasant cottage, conveniently neat,
With a mill and some meadows – a freehold estate,
A well-meaning miller by labour supplies
Those blessings that grandeur to the great ones denies:

No passions to plague him, no cares to torment,
His constant companions are health and content;
Their lordships in lace may remark if they will,
He's honest tho' daub'd with the dust of his mill.

Ere the lark's early carrols salute the new day
He springs from his cottage as jocund as May;
He cheerfully whistles, regardless of care,
Or sings the last ballad he bought at the fair:

While courtiers are toil'd in the cobwebs of state,
Or bribing elections in hopes to be great,
No fraud, or ambition his bosom does fill,
Contented he works, if there's grist for his mill.

On Sunday bedeck'd in his homespun array,
At church he's the loudest, to chaunt or to pray:
He sits to a dinner of plain English food,
'Tho' simple the pudding, his appetite's good.

At night, when the priest and exciseman are gone,
He quaffs at the alehouse with Roger and John,
Then reels to his pillow, and dreams of no ill;
No monarch more blest than the man of the mill.

John Cunningham
(1729–1773)

A Hand in the Bird

I'm a maiden who is forty,
And a maiden I shall stay.
There are some who call me haughty,
But I care not what they say.

I was running the tombola
At our church bazaar today,
And doing it with gusto
In my usual jolly way....

When suddenly, I knew not why,
There came a funny feeling
Of something *crawling up my thigh*
I nearly hit the ceiling!

A mouse! I though. How foul! How mean!
How exquisitely tickly!
Quite soon I know I'm going to scream.
I've got to catch it quickly.

I made a grab. I caught the mouse,
Now right inside my knickers.
A mouse my foot! It was a HAND!
Great Scott! It was the vicar's!

Roald Dahl
(1916–1990)

Sheep in the Cotswolds

from: Poly-Olbion

And, now that everything may in the proper place
Most aptly be contriv'd, the sheep our Wold doth breed
(The simplest though it seem) shall our description need,
And shepherd-like, the Muse thus of that kind doth speak:
No brown, nor sullied black the face or legs doth streak,
Like those of Moreland, Cank, or of the Cambrian Hills
That lightly laden are: but Cotswold wisely fills
Her with the whitest kind: whose brows so woolly be,
As men in her fair sheep no emptiness should see.
The staple deep and thick, through, to the very grain,
Most strongly keepeth out the violentest rain:
A body long and large, the buttocks equal broad;
As fit to undergo the full and weighty load.
And of the fleecy face, the flank doth nothing lack,
But everywhere is stor'd; the belly, as the back.
The fair and goodly flock, the shepherd's only pride,
As white as winter's snow, when from the river's side
He drives his new-wash'd sheep; or on the shearing-day,
When as the lusty ram, with those rich spoils of May
His crooked horns hath crown'd; the bell-wether, so brave
As none in all the flock they like themselves would have.

Michael Drayton
(1563–1631)

Elegy Written in a Country Churchyard

Verses 1–9

The curfew tolls the knell of parting day,
The lowing herd wind slowly o'er the lea,
The plowman homeward plods his weary way,
And leaves the world to darkness and to me.

Now fades the glimmering landscape on the sight,
And all the air a solemn stillness holds,
Save where the beetle wheels his droning flight,
And drowsy tinklings lull the distant folds;

Save that from yonder ivy-mantled tow'r
The mopeing owl does to the moon complain
Of such, as wand'ring near her secret bow'r,
Molest her ancient solitary reign.

Beneath those rugged elms, that yew-tree's shade,
Where heaves the turf in many a mould'ring heap,
Each in his narrow cell for ever laid,
The rude Forefathers of the hamlet sleep.

The breezy call of incense-breathing Morn,
The swallow twitt'ring from the straw-built shed,
The cock's shrill clarion, or the ecchoing horn,
No more shall rouse them from their lowly bed.

For them no more the blazing hearth shall burn,
Or busy housewife ply her evening care:
No children run to lisp their sire's return,
Or climb his knees the envied kiss to share.

Oft did the harvest to their sickle yield,
Their furrow oft the stubborn glebe has broke;
How jocund did they drive their team afield!
How bow'd the woods beneath their sturdy stroke!

Let not Ambition mock their useful toil,
Their homely joys, and destiny obscure;
Nor grandeur hear with a disdainful smile,
The short and simple annals of the poor.

The boast of heraldry, the pomp of pow'r,
And all that beauty, all that wealth e'er gave,
Await alike th' inevitable hour.
The paths of glory lead but to the grave.

Thomas Gray
(1716–1771)

To Meddowes

from: Hesperides

Ye have been fresh and green,
    Ye have been fill'd with flowers:
And ye the Walks have been
    Where Maids have spent their houres.

You have beheld, how they
    With *Wicker Arks* did come
To kisse, and beare away
    The richer Couslips home.

Y'ave heard them sweetly sing,
    And seen them in a Round:
Each Virgin, like a Spring,
    With Hony-succles crown'd,

But now, we see, none here,
    Whose silv'rie feet did tread,
And with dishevell'd Haire,
    Adorn'd this smoother Mead.

Like Unthrifts, having spent,
    Your stock, and needy grown,
Y'are left here to lament
    Your poore estates, alone.

Robert Herrick
(1591–1674)

English Wild Flowers

Forget the Latin names; the English ones
Are gracious and specific. Hedge-rows are
Quickening fast with vetch and cow-parsley.
And fast along the lawn the daisies rise
For chains or for the murdering lawn-mower.

Look everywhere, there is all botany
Laid between rising corn,
Infesting hay-fields. Look, the buttercup
Stares at the sun and seems to take a share
Of wealthy light. It glows beneath our chins.

Slim shepherd's purse is lost in dandelions,
Scabious will show a little later. See,
The dog-rose in the hedge. It dies at once
When you pluck it. Forget-me-nots disclose
Points of pure blue, the sovereign blue of sky.
And then there are the herbs.

Counting this floral beauty I grow warm
With patriotism. These are my own flowers,
Springing to pleasant life in my own nation.
The times are dark but never too dark for
An Eden Summer, this flower-rich creation.

Elizabeth Jennings
(1926–2001)

Blackberrying

Nobody in the lane, and nothing, nothing but blackberries,
Blackberries on either side, though on the right mainly,
A blackberry alley, going down in hooks, and a sea
Somewhere at the end of it, heaving. Blackberries
Big as the ball of my thumb, and dumb as eyes
Ebon in the hedges, fat
With blue-red juices. These they squander on my fingers.
I had not asked for such a blood sisterhood; they must love me.
They accommodate themselves to my milkbottle, flattening their
    sides.

Overhead go the choughs in black, cacophonous flocks –
Bits of burnt paper wheeling in a blown sky.
Theirs is the only voice, protesting, protesting.
I do not think the sea will appear at all.
The high, green meadows are glowing, as if lit from within.
I come to one bush of berries so ripe it is a bush of flies,
Hanging their bluegreen bellies and their wing panes in a Chinese
    screen.
The honey-feast of the berries has stunned them; they believe they are
    in heaven.
One more hook, and the berries and bushes end.

The only thing to come now is the sea.
From between two hills a sudden wind funnels at me,
Slapping its phantom laundry in my face.
These hills are too green and sweet to have tasted salt.
I follow the sheep path between them. A last hook brings me
To the hills' northern face, and the face is orange rock
That looks out on nothing, nothing but a great space
Of white and pewter lights, and a din like silversmiths
Beating and beating at an intractable metal.

Sylvia Plath
(1932–1963)

84

The Weald of Kent

from: The Land

The common saying goes, that on the hill
A man may lie in bed to work his farm,
Propping his elbows on his window-sill
To watch his harvest growing like a charm.
But the man who works the wet and weeping soil
Down in the Weald, must marl and delve and till
His three-horse land, fearing nor sweat nor droil.
For through the winter he must fight the flood,
The clay, that yellow enemy, that rots
His land, sucks at his horses' hooves
So that his waggon plunges in the mud,
And horses strain, but waggon never moves;
Delays his plough, and holds his spud
With heavy spite in trenching garden-plots;
The catchy clay, that does its utmost harm,
And comes into his house, to spoil
Even his dwelling, creeps into his bones
Before their time, and makes them ache,
Leaving its token in his husky tones;
And all through summer he must see the clay
Harden as brick and bake,
And open cracks to swallow up his arm,
Where neither harrow, hoe, nor rake
Can rasp a tilth, but young and eager shoots
Pierce into blank, and wither at the roots.
Yet with his stupid loyalty he will say,
Being a wealden man of wealden land,
Holding his wealden honour as a pledge,

'In times of drought those farms up on the ridge,
Light soil, half sand,
With the first summer gale blow half away,'
And lifts his eyes towards the hills with scorn.

Vita Sackville-West
(1892–1962)

Haymaking

After night's thunder far away had rolled
The fiery day had a kernel sweet of cold,
And in the perfect blue the clouds uncurled,
Like the first gods before they made the world
And misery, swimming the stormless sea
In beauty and in divine gaiety.
The smooth white empty road was lightly strewn
With leaves – the holly's Autumn falls in June –
And fir cones standing up stiff in the heat.
The mill-foot water tumbled white and lit
With tossing crystals, happier than any crowd
Of children pouring out of school aloud.
And in the little thickets where a sleeper
For ever might lie lost, the nettle creeper
And garden-warbler sang unceasingly;
While over them shrill shrieked in his fierce glee
The swift with wings and tail as sharp and narrow
As if the bow had flown off with the arrow.
Only the scent of woodbine and hay new mown
Travelled down the road. In the field sloping down,
Park-like, to where its willows showed the brook,
Haymakers rested. The tosser lay forsook
Out in the sun; and the long waggon stood
Without its team: it seemed it never would
Move from the shadow of that single yew.
The team, as still, until their task was due,
Beside the labourers enjoyed the shade
That three squat oaks mid-field together made
Upon a circle of grass and weed uncut,
And on the hollow, once a chalk pit, but

Now brimmed with nut and elder-flower so clean.
The men leaned on their rakes, about to begin,
But still. And all were silent. All was old,
This morning time, with a great age untold,
Older than Clare and Cobbett, Morland and Crome,
Than, at the field's far edge, the farmer's home,
A white house crouched at the foot of a great tree.
Under the heavens that know not what years be
The men, the beasts, the trees, the implements
Uttered even what they will in times far hence –
All of us gone out of the reach of change –
Immortal in a picture of an old grange.

Edward Thomas
(1878–1917)

Ivied Walls
and Mullioned
Windows

To Mrs Boteler

A description of her garden

How charming is this little spot
  Disposed with art and taste,
A thousand beauties intermixed
  Prepare the eyes a feast.

The lovely limes in ample rows
  With woodbines climbing round,
A shining gravel walk enclose
  Where not a weed is found.

The crocus, primrose, daffodil,
  And cowslip sweet I sing,
And fragrant purple violet –
  All harbingers of spring;

The musky lovely blushing pink,
  Jonquil with rich perfume,
Tulips that vie with Iris' bow,
  And balsam's annual bloom;

The immortal pea, fair 'emone,
  And beamy marigold,
And polyanthus (lovely tribe!)
  Their various blooms unfold.

The gardener's pride, ranunculus,
    Bell-flower ethereal blue,
The rose campion, and golden lupe,
    And wonder of Peru;

The amaranths, as poets sing,
    That Juno deigned to wear,
That in Hesperian gardens spring,
    Bloom fair and fragrant here.

The lily fair as new-fallen snow:
    All these the borders grace,
And myrtles, roses, jessamines
    With fragrance fill the place.

A group of dwarfish apple trees
    Appear, a fairy scene,
Laden with fruit – such Paris gave
    To Venus, beauty's queen.

Stately the rising mount appears
    With towering elms overspread,
Whose gently waving branches form
    At noon a cooling shade.

The laurel plant, the victor's crown,
    And bays by poets worn,
The particoloured phillyrea
    And May-performing thorn –

These line the walks and make the bounds
    All verdant, young, and fair:
All speak the owner's judgement good
    And praise the gardener's care.

Faint emblem of a fairer mind
    That over all presides:
For every virtue's planted there,
    And every action guides.

Mary Chandler
(1687–1745)

A Country Mansion

This ancient house so notable
For its gables and great staircase,
Its mulberry-trees and alleys of clipped yew,
Humbles the show of every near demesne.

At the beginning it acknowledged owners –
Father, son, grandson –
But then, surviving the last heirs of the line,
Became a place for life-tenancy only.

At the beginning, no hint of fate,
No rats and no haunting;
In the garden, then, fruit-trees grew
Slender and similar in long rows.

A bedroom with a low ceiling
Caused little fret at first;
But gradual generations of discomfort
Have bred an anger there to stifle sleep.

And the venerable dining-room,
Where port in Limerick glasses
Glows twice as red reflected
In the memory-mirror of the waxed table –

For a time with paint and flowered paper
A mistress tamed its walls,
But pious antiquarian hands, groping,
Rediscovered the grey panels beneath.

Children love the old house tearfully,
And the parterres, how fertile!
Married couples under the testers hugging
Enjoy carnality's bliss as nowhere else.

A smell of mould from loft to cellar,
Yet sap still brisk in the oak
Of the great beams: if ever they use a saw
It will stain, as cutting a branch from a green tree.

. . . Old Parr had lived one hundred and five
(So to King Charles he bragged)
When he did open penance, in a sheet,
For fornication with posterity.

Old Parr died; not so the mansion
Whose inhabitants, bewitched,
Pour their fresh blood through its historic veins
And, if a tile blow from the roof, tremble.

The last-born of this race of sacristans
Broke the long spell, departed;
They lay his knife and fork at every meal
And every evening warm his bed;

Yet cannot draw him back from the far roads
For trifling by the lily-pool
Or wine at the hushed table where they meet,
The guests of genealogy.

It was his childhood's pleasure-ground
And still may claim his corpse,
Yet foster-cradle or foster-grave
He will not count as home.

This rebel does not hate the house,
Nor its dusty joys impugn:
No place less reverend could provoke
So proud an absence from it.

He has that new malaise of time:
Gratitude choking with vexation
That he should opulently inherit
The goods and titles of the extinct.

Robert Graves
(1895–1985)

Architectural Masks

I

There is a house with ivied walls,
And mullioned windows worn and old,
And the long dwellers in those halls
Have souls that know but sordid calls,
    And daily dote on gold.

II

In blazing brick and plated show
Not far away a 'villa' gleams,
And here a family few may know,
With book and pencil, viol and bow,
    Lead inner lives of dreams.

III

The philosophic passers say,
'See that old mansion mossed and fair,
Poetic souls therein are they:
And O that gaudy box! Away,
    You vulgar people there.'

Thomas Hardy
(1840–1928)

The Homes of England

The stately homes of England,
    How beautiful they stand!
Amidst their tall ancestral trees,
    O'er all the pleasant land.
The deer across their greensward bound
    Thro' shade and sunny gleam,
And the swan glides past them with the sound
    Of some rejoicing stream.

The merry homes of England!
    Around their hearths by night,
What gladsome looks of household love
    Meet in the ruddy light!
There woman's voice flows forth in song,
    Or childhood's tale is told,
Or lips move tunefully along
    Some glorious page of old.

The blessed homes of England!
    How softly on their bowers
Is laid the holy quietness
    That breathes from Sabbath hours!
Solemn, yet sweet, the church-bell's chime
    Floats thro' their woods at morn;
All other sounds, in that still time,
    Of breeze and leaf are born.

The cottage homes of England!
    By thousands on her plains,
They are smiling o'er the silvery brooks,

And round the hamlet fanes.
Through glowing orchards forth they peep,
 Each from its nook of leaves,
And fearless there the lowly sleep,
 As the bird beneath the eaves.

The free, fair homes of England!
 Long, long, in hut and hall,
May hearts of native proof be rear'd
 To guard each hallow'd wall!
And green for ever be the groves,
 And bright the flowery sod,
Where first the child's glad spirit loves
 Its country and its God!

Dorothea Felicia Hemans
(1793–1835)

To Penshurst

Lines 1–14

Thou art not, PENSHURST, built to envious show,
    Of touch, or marble; nor canst boast a row
Of polish'd pillars, or a roofe of gold:
    Thou hast no lantherne, whereof tales are told;
Or stayre, or courts, but stand'st an ancient pile,
    And these grudg'd at, art reverenc'd the while.
Thou joy'st in better markes, of soyle, of ayre,
    Of wood, of water: therein thou art faire.
Thou hast thy walkes for health, as well as sport:
    Thy *Mount*, to which the *Dryads* doe resort,
Where PAN, and BACCHUS their high feasts have made,
    Beneath the broad beech, and the chestnut shade;
That taller tree, which of a nut was set,
    At his great birth, where all the *Muses* met.

Ben Jonson
(1572–1637)

The Glory of the Garden

Our England is a garden that is full of stately views,
Of borders, beds and shrubberies and lawns and avenues,
With statues on the terraces and peacocks strutting by;
But the Glory of the Garden lies in more than meets the eye.

For where the old thick laurels grow, along the thin red wall,
You find the tool- and potting-sheds which are the heart of all;
The cold-frames and the hot-houses, the dungpits and the tanks,
The rollers, carts and drain-pipes, with the barrows and the planks.

And there you'll see the gardeners, the men and 'prentice boys
Told off to do as they are bid and do it without noise;
For, except when seeds are planted and we shout to scare the birds,
The Glory of the Garden it abideth not in words.

And some can pot begonias and some can bud a rose,
And some are hardly fit to trust with anything that grows;
But they can roll and trim the lawns and sift the sand and loam,
For the Glory of the Garden occupieth all who come.

Our England is a garden, and such gardens are not made
By singing: – 'Oh, how beautiful!' and sitting in the shade,
While better men than we go out and start their working lives
At grubbing weeds from gravel-paths with broken dinner-knives.

There's not a pair of legs so thin, there's not a head so thick,
There's not a hand so weak and white, nor yet a heart so sick,
But it can find some needful job that's crying to be done,
For the Glory of the Garden glorifieth everyone.

Then seek your job with thankfulness and work till further orders,
If it's only netting strawberries or killing slugs in borders;
And when your back stops aching and your hands begin to harden,
You will find yourself a partner in the Glory of the Garden.

Oh, Adam was a gardener, and God who made him sees
That half a proper gardener's work is done upon his knees,
So when your work is finished, you can wash your hands and pray
For the Glory of the Garden, that it may not pass away!
And the Glory of the Garden it shall never pass away!

Rudyard Kipling
(1865–1936)

Upon Appleton House, to my Lord Fairfax

Verses LXIII, LXIV

When first the Eye this Forrest sees
It seems indeed as *Wood* not *Trees:*
As if their neighbourhood so old
To one great Trunk them all did mold.
There the huge Bulk takes place, as ment
To thrust up a *Fifth Element;*
And stretches still so closely wedg'd
As if the Night within were hedg'd.

Dark all without it knits; within
It opens passable and thin;
And in as loose an order grows,
As the *Corinthian Porticoes.*
The arching Boughs unite between
The Columnes of the Temple green;
And underneath the winged Quires
Echo about their tuned Fires.

Andrew Marvell
(1621–1678)

The Choice

Lines 1–34

If heav'n the grateful liberty would give,
That I might choose my method how to live,
And all those hours propitious Fate should lend
In blissful ease and satisfaction spend:
     Near some fair town I'd have a private seat,
Built uniform, not little, nor too great:
Better, if on a rising ground it stood,
Fields on this side, on that a neighbouring wood.
It should within no other things contain
But what were useful, necessary, plain:
Methinks 'tis nauseous, and I'd ne'er endure
The needless pomp of gaudy furniture.
A little garden, grateful to the eye,
And a cool rivulet run murm'ring by,
On whose delicious banks a stately row
Of shady limes or sycamores should grow;
At th'end of which a silent study placed
Should be with all the noblest authors graced:
Horace and Virgil, in whose mighty lines
Immortal wit and solid learning shines;
Sharp Juvenal, and am'rous Ovid too,
Who all the turns of love's soft passion knew;
He that with judgement reads his charming lines,
In which strong art with stronger nature joins,
Must grant his fancy does the best excel,
His thoughts so tender, and expressed so well;
With all those moderns, men of steady sense,
Esteemed for learning and for eloquence,
In some of these, as fancy should advise,

I'd always take my morning exercise:
For sure no minutes bring us more content
Than those in pleasing, useful studies spent.
    I'd have a clear and competent estate,
That I might live genteely, but not great.

John Pomfret
(1667–1702)

Upon the Duke of Marlborough's House at Woodstock

(Blenheim Palace)

'Atria longa patent; sed nec cœnantibus usquam,
Nec somno, locus est: quam bene non habitas'
Martial, *Epigr (XII, 50, vv. 7, 8)*

See, sir, here's the grand approach;
This way is for his Grace's coach:
There lies the bridge, and here's the clock,
Observe the lion and the cock,
The spacious court, the colonnade,
And mark how wide the hall is made!
The chimneys are so well design'd,
They never smoke in any wind.
This gallery's contrived for walking,
The windows to retire and talk in;
The council chamber for debate,
And all the rest are rooms of state.
　　　Thanks, sir, cried I, 'tis very fine,
But where d'ye sleep, or where d'ye dine?
I find, by all you have been telling,
That 'tis a house, but not a dwelling.

Alexander Pope
(1688–1744)

Sandwiches
and Flasks

Foote Ball

from: The Fifth Eclogue

Eche time and season hath his delite and joyes,
Loke in the streets beholde the little boyes,
Howe in fruite season for ioy they sing and hop,
In lent is eche one full busy with his top,
And nowe in winter for all the greevous colde
All rent and ragged a man may them beholde,
They have great pleasour supposing well to dine,
When men be busied in killing of fat swine,
They get the bladder and blowe it great and thin,
With many beanes or peason put within,
It ratleth, soundeth, and shineth clere and fayre,
While it is throwen and caste up in the ayre,
Eche one contendeth and hath a great delite
With foote and with hande the bladder for to smite,
If it fall on the grounde they lifte it up agayne,
This wise to labour they count it for no payne,
Renning and leaping they drive away the colde.
The sturdie plowmen lustie, strong and bold
Overcommeth the winter with driving the foote ball,
Forgetting labour and many a grievous fall.

Alexander Barclay
(1475?–1552)

Hunter Trials

It's awf'lly bad luck on Diana,
    Her ponies have swallowed their bits;
She fished down their throats with a spanner
    And frightened them all into fits.

So now she's attempting to borrow
    Do lend her some bits, Mummy, *do*;
I'll lend her my own for to-morrow,
    But to-day *I'll* be wanting them too.

Just look at Prunella on Guzzle,
    The wizardest pony on earth;
Why doesn't she slacken his muzzle
    And tighten the breech in his girth?

I say, Mummy, there's Mrs. Geyser
    And doesn't she look pretty sick?
I bet it's because Mona Lisa
    Was hit on the hock with a brick.

Miss Blewitt says Monica threw it,
    But Monica says it was Joan,
And Joan's very thick with Miss Blewitt,
    So Monica's sulking alone.

And Margaret failed in her paces,
    Her withers got tied in a noose,
So her coronets caught in the traces
    And now all her fetlocks are loose.

Oh, it's me now. I'm terribly nervous.
  I wonder if Smudges will shy.
She's practically certain to swerve as
  Her Pelham is over one eye.

*   *   *   *   *

Oh wasn't it naughty of Smudges?
  Oh, Mummy. I'm sick with disgust.
She threw me in front of the Judges,
  And my silly old collarbone's bust.

John Betjeman
(1906–1984)

Summer Beach

For how long known this boundless wash of light,
    This smell of purity, this gleaming waste,
This wind? This brown, strewn wrack how old a sight,
    These pebbles round to touch and salt to taste.

See, the slow marbled heave, the liquid arch,
    Before the waves' procession to the land
Flowers in foam; the ripples' onward march,
    Their last caresses on the pure hard sand.

For how long known these bleaching corks, new-made
    Smooth and enchanted from the lapping sea?
Since I first laboured with a wooden spade
    Against this background of Eternity.

Frances Cornford
(1886–1960)

Fishing

from: Rural Sports: A Georgic Inscribed to Mr. Pope

When genial spring a living warmth bestows,
And o'er the year her verdant mantle throws,
No swelling inundation hides the grounds;
But crystal currents glide within their bounds;
The finny brood their wonted haunts forsake,
Float in the sun, and skim along the lake,
With frequent leap they range the shallow streams,
Their silver coats reflect the dazzling beams.
Now let the fisherman his tolls prepare,
And arm himself with every watery snare;
His hooks, his lines persue with careful eye,
Increase his tackle, and his rod retye.

When floating clouds their spongy fleeces drain,
Troubling the streams with swift-descending rain,
And waters, tumbling down the mountain's side,
Bear the loose soil into the swelling tide;
Then, soon as vernal gales begin to rise,
And drive the liquid burthen through the skies,
The fisher to the neighb'ring current speeds,
Whose rapid surface purls, unknown to weeds;
Upon a rising border of the brook
He sits him down, and ties the treach'rous hook;
Now expectation chears his eager thought,
His bosom glows with treasures yet uncaught,
Before his eyes a banquet seems to stand,
Where every guest applauds his skilful hand.

John Gay
(1685–1732)

A Tennis-court

from: Phyala Lachrymarum

Dopo il Giuco, cosi van el sacco il Re, come il pedone

If in my weak conceit, (for selfe disport),
The world I sample to a Tennis-court,
Where fate and fortune daily meet to play,
I doe conceive, I doe not much misse-say.

All manner chance are Rackets, wherewithal
They bandie men, from wall to wall;
Some over Lyne, to honour and great place,
Some under Lyne, to inflame and disgrace;
Some with a cutting stroke they nimbly sent
Into the hazard placed at the end;
Resembling well the rest which all they have,
Whom death hath seiz'd, and placed in their grave:
Some o're the wall they bandie quite away,
Who never more are seen to come in play:
Which intimates that even the very best
Are soone forgot of all, if once deceast.

So, (whether silke-quilt ball it bee, or whether
Made of coarse cloth, or of most homely letther;)
They all alike are banded to and fro,
And all at last to selfe same end do goe,
Where is no difference, or strife for place,
No odds between a Trype-wife and your Grace;
The penny-counter's every whit as good
As that which in the place of thousands stood.

William Lathum

(fl. 1634)

Skating in the Evening

from: The Prelude

And in the frosty season, when the sun
Was set, and visible for many a mile
The cottage windows blazed through the twilight gloom,
I heeded not their summons: happy time
It was indeed for all of us – for me
It was a time of rapture! Clear and loud
The village clock tolled six, – I wheeled about,
Proud and exalting like an untired horse
That cares not for his home. All shod with steel.
We hissed along the polished ice in games
Confederate, imitative of the chase
And woodland pleasures, – the resounding horn,
The pack loud chiming, and the hunted hare.
So through the darkness and the cold we flew,
And not a voice was idle; with the din
Smitten, the precipices rang aloud;
The leafless trees and every icy crag
Tinkled like iron; while far distant hills
Into the tumult sent an alien sound
Of melancholy not unnoticed, while the stars
Eastward were sparkling clear, and in the west
The orange sky of evening died away.
Not seldom from the uproar I retired
Into a silent bay, or sportively
Glanced sideway, leaving the tumultuous throng,
To cut across the reflex of a star
That fled, and, flying still before me, gleamed
Upon the glassy plain; and oftentimes,
When we had given our bodies to the wind,

And all the shadowy banks on either side
Came sweeping through the darkness, spinning still
The rapid line of motion, then at once
Have I, reclining back upon my heels,
Stopped short; yet still the solitary cliffs
Wheeled by me – even as if the earth had rolled
With visible motion her diurnal round!
Behind me they did stretch in solemn train,
Feebler and feebler, and I stood and watched
Till all was tranquil as in a dreamless sleep.

William Wordsworth
(1770–1850)

Test Match at Lords

Bailey bowling, McLean cuts him late for one.
I walk from the Long Room into the slanting sun.
Two ramrod ancients halt as Statham starts his run.
Then, elbows linked, but straight as sailors
On a tilting deck, they move. One, square-shouldered as a tailor's
Model, leans over, whispering in the other's ear:
'Go easy. Steps here. This end bowling.'
Turning, I watch Barnes guide Rhodes into fresher air,
As if to continue an innings, though Rhodes may only play by ear.

Alan Ross
(1922–2001)

A Day on the River

It moved so slowly, friendly as a dog
Whose teeth would never bite;
It licked the hand with cool and gentle tongue
And seemed to share its parasites' delight
Who moved upon its back or moored among
The hairy shallows overhung
With natural parasols of leaves
And bubbling birdsong.
Ukuleles twanged and ladies sang
In punts and houseboats vivid as our own
Bold paintings of the Ark;
This was summer's self to any child:
The plop and suck of water and the old
Sweet rankness in the air beguiled
With deft archaic spells the dim
Deliberations of the land,
Dear river, comforting
More than the trailing hand.

The afternoon of sandwiches and flasks
Drifted away.
The breeze across the shivering water grew
Perceptibly in strength. The sun began to bleed.

'Time to go home,' the punctured uncles said,
And back on land
We trembled at the river's faint, low growl
And as the birds probed the mutilated sky
We knew that, with the night,
The river's teeth grew sharp
And they could bite.

Vernon Scannell
(1922–2007)

In the
Perfect Blue
the Clouds
Uncurled

Spring Quiet

Gone were but the Winter,
    Come were but the Spring,
I would go to a covert
    Where the birds sing;

Where in the whitethorn
    Singeth a thrush
And a robin sings
    In the holly-bush.

Full of fresh scents
    Are the budding boughs
Arching high over
    A cool green house:

Full of sweet scents,
    And whispering air
Which sayeth softly:
    "We spread no snare;

"Here dwell in safety,
    Here dwell alone,
With a clear stream
    And a mossy stone.

"Here the sun shineth
    Most shadily;
Here is heard an echo
    Of the far sea,
    Tho' far off it be."

Christina Rossetti
(1830–1894)

Loveliest of Trees

A Shropshire Lad II

Loveliest of trees, the cherry now
Is hung with bloom along the bough,
And stands about the woodland ride
Wearing white for Eastertide.

Now, of my threescore years and ten,
Twenty will not come again,
And take from seventy springs a score,
It only leaves me fifty more.

And since to look at things in bloom
Fifty springs are little room,
About the woodlands I will go
To see the cherry hung with snow.

A. E. Housman
(1859- 1936)

Summer Tints

How sweet I've wandered bosom-deep in grain,
When Summer's mellowing pencil sweeps his shades
Of ripening tinges o'er the checkered plain:
Light tawny oat-lands wi' their yellow blades;
And bearded corn like armies on parade;
Beans lightly scorched that still preserved their green;
And nodding lands of wheat in bleachy brown;
And streaking banks, where many a maid and clown
Contrasts a sweetness to the rural scene,
Forming the little haycocks up and down,
While o'er the face of nature softly swept
The lingering wind, mixing the brown and green,
So sweet that shepherds from their bowers have crept
And stood delighted musing o'er the scene.

John Clare
(1793–1864)

Summer and Winter

It was a bright and cheerful afternoon,
Towards the end of the sunny month of June,
When the north wind congregates in crowds
The floating mountains of the silver clouds
From the horizon – and the stainless sky
Opens beyond them like eternity.
All things rejoiced beneath the sun; the weeds,
The river, and the corn-fields, and the reeds;
The willow leaves that glanced in the light breeze,
And the firm foliage of the larger trees.

It was a winter such as when birds die
In the deep forests; and fishes lie
Stiffened in the translucent ice, which makes
Even the mud and slime of the warm lakes
A wrinkled clod as hard a brick; and when,
Among their children, comfortable men
Gather about great fires, and yet feel cold:
Alas, then, for the homeless beggar old!

Percy Bysshe Shelley
(1792–1822)

The Harvest Moon

The flame-red moon, the harvest moon,
Rolls along the hills, gently bouncing,
A vast balloon,
Till it takes off, and sinks upward
To lie in the bottom of the sky, like a gold doubloon.

The harvest moon has come,
Booming softly through heaven, like a bassoon.
And earth replies all night, like a deep drum.

So people can't sleep,
So they go out where elms and oak trees keep
A kneeling vigil, in a religious hush.
The harvest moon has come!

And all the moonlit cows and all the sheep
Stare up at her petrified, while she swells
Filling heaven, as if red hot, and sailing
Closer and closer like the end of the world.

Till the gold fields of stiff wheat
Cry 'We are ripe, reap us!' and the rivers
Sweat from the melting hills.

Ted Hughes
(1930–1998)

To Autumn

I

Season of mists and mellow fruitfulness,
    Close bosom-friend of the maturing sun;
Conspiring with him how to load and bless
    With fruit the vines that round the thatch-eves run;
To bend with apples the moss'd cottage-trees,
    And fill all fruit with ripeness to the core;
        To swell the gourd, and plump the hazel shells
    With a sweet kernel; to set budding more,
And still more, later flowers for the bees,
Until they think warm days will never cease,
    For Summer has o'er-brimmed their clammy cells.

II

Who hath not seen thee oft amid thy store?
    Sometimes whoever seeks abroad may find
Thee sitting careless on a granary floor,
    Thy hair soft-lifted by the winnowing wind;
Or on a half-reaped furrow sound asleep,
    Drows'd with the fume of poppies, while thy hook
        Spares the next swathe and all its twined flowers:
And sometimes like a gleaner thou dost keep
    Steady thy laden head across a brook;
    Or by a cyder-press, with patient look,
        Thou watchest the last oozing hours by hours.

III

Where are the songs of Spring? Ay, where are they?
    Think not of them, thou hast thy music too, –
While barred clouds bloom the soft-dying day,

And touch the stubble-plains with rosy hue;
Then in a wailful choir the small gnats mourn
  Among the river sallows, borne aloft
    Or sinking as the light wind lives or dies;
And full-grown lambs loud bleat from hilly bourn;
  Hedge-crickets sing; and now with treble soft
  The red-breast whistles from a garden-croft;
    And gathering swallows twitter in the skies.

John Keats
(1795–1821)

No!

No sun – no moon!
No morn – no noon –
No dawn – no dusk – no proper time of day –
No sky – no earthly view –
No distance looking blue –
No road – no street – no 't'other side the way' –
No end to any Row –
No indications where the Crescents go –
No top to any steeple –
No recognitions of familiar people –
No courtesies for showing 'em –
No knowing 'em! –
No travelling at all – no locomotion,
No inkling of the way – no notion –
'No go' – by land or ocean –
No mail – no post –
No news from any foreign coast –
No Park – no Ring – no afternoon gentility –
No company – no nobility –
No warmth, no cheerfulness, no healthful ease,
No comfortable feel in any member –
No shade, no shine, no butterflies, no bees,
No fruits, no flowers, no leaves, no birds, –
November!

Thomas Hood
(1799–1845)

At Middle-Field Gate in February

The bars are thick with drops that show
    As they gather themselves from the fog
Like silver buttons ranged in a row,
And as evenly spaced as if measured, although
    They fall at the feeblest jog.

They load the leafless hedge hard by,
    And the blades of last year's grass,
While the fallow ploughland turned up nigh
In raw rolls clammy and clogging lie –
    Too clogging for feet to pass.

How dry it was on a far-back day
    When straws hung the hedge and around,
When amid the sheaves in amorous play
In curtained bonnets and light array
    Bloomed a bevy now underground!

Thomas Hardy
(1840–1928)

Spring and Winter

from: Love's Labours Lost Act V scene ii

SPRING

When daisies pied and violets blue,
 And lady-smocks, all silver-white,
And cuckoo-buds of yellow hue
 Do paint the meadows with delight,
The cuckoo then, on every tree,
Mocks married men; for thus sings he,
 Cuckoo!
Cuckoo, cuckoo! – O word of fear,
Unpleasing to a married ear!

When shepherds pipe on oaten straws,
 And merry larks are ploughmen's clocks;
When turtles tread, and rooks and daws,
 And maidens bleach their summer smocks,
The cuckoo then on every tree
Mocks married men; for thus sings he,
 Cuckoo!
Cuckoo, cuckoo! – O word of fear
Unpleasing to a married ear.

WINTER

When icicles hang by the wall,
 And Dick the shepherd blows his nail;
And Tom bears logs into the hall,
 And milk comes frozen home in pail;
When blood is nipp'd, and ways be foul,
Then nightly sings the staring owl,

Tu-whit, tu-whoo! – a merry note,
While greasy Joan doth keel the pot.

When all aloud the wind doth blow,
    And coughing drowns the parson's saw:
And birds sit brooding in the snow,
    And Marian's nose looks red and raw;
When roasted crabs hiss in the bowl,
Then nightly sings the staring owl,
Tu-whit, tu-whoo! – a merry note,
While greasy Joan doth keel the pot.

William Shakespeare
(1564–1616)

Only in England

The English Race

from: The True-Born Englishman

The *Romans* first with *Julius Caesar* came,
Including all the Nations of that Name,
Gauls, *Greeks*, and *Lombards*; and by Computation,
Auxiliaries or Slaves of ev'ry Nation.
With *Hengist, Saxons*; *Danes* with *Sueno* came,
In search of Plunder, not in search of Fame.
Scots, *Picts*, and *Irish* from th' Hibernian Shore:
And Conqu'ring *William* brought the *Normans* o're.

    All these their Barb'rous Offspring left behind,
The Dregs of Armies, they of all Mankind;
Blended with *Britains* who before were here,
Of whom the *Welsh* ha' blest the Character.

    From this Amphibious Ill-born Mob began
That vain ill-natured thing, an Englishman.
The Customs, Sirnames, Languages, and Manners,
Of all these Nations are their own Explainers:
Whose Relicks are so lasting and so strong,
They ha' left a *Shiboleth* upon our Tongue;
By which with easy search you may distinguish
Your *Roman-Saxon-Danish-Norman* English.

Daniel Defoe
(1660–1731)

Saint George and the Dragon

Saint George he slew the dragon,
    But he didn't shout hurray.
He dumped it in the wagon
    Just to clear the mess away.

But the waggoner he sold it
    To a showman at the fair
And when Saint George was told it,
    He was almost in despair.

For the people crowded round it
    To admire its teeth and claws,
But Saint George he was an Englishman
    And did not like applause.

"The creechah weighed a ton at most,"
    He muttered through his vizahd,
"I do not feel inclined to boast
    About that puny lizahd."

Alfred Noyes
(1880–1958)

The Corner Shop

I remember it away from London
In the English midlands of mines and pottery kilns
And vowels as flat as the earth
Aroung Nuneaton. But Leicestershire,
Warwickshire, or Derby – what does it matter?
All corner shops are alike and all unlike
All other shops: only they can nourish
The growing boy – it may be sherbet
Suckers and dabs, straps of liquorice,
Ice cream cornets or aniseed,
Or it may be an envelope sealed
Off from the innocent eye and beginning
The end of innocence, or it may be
Sweet cigarettes to swank with and swallow,
Or marbles and tops mixed up
In a jumble sale where comic
Postcards scorch the face that goes too near
And string is chewing gum and chewing gum
Elastic and elastic is the corner
Departmental store and tobacconist,
Bookseller, grocer, universal provider
Of food for thought to the boy
Who visits it daily and wonders
What is around the corner.

Clifford Dyment
(1914–1971)

The Museum

from: The Pitt-Rivers Museum, Oxford

Is shut
22 hours a day and all day Sunday
And should not be confused
With its academic brother, full of fossils
And skeletons of bearded seals. Take
Your heart in your hand and go; it does not sport
Any of Ruskin's hothouse Venetian
And resembles rather, with its dusty girders,
A vast gymnasium or barracks   though
The resemblance ends where

Entering
You will find yourself in a climate of nut castanets,
A musical whip
From the Torres Straits, from Mirzapur a sistrum
Called Jumka, 'used by aboriginal
Tribes to attract small game
On dark nights', a mute violin,
Whistling arrows, coolie cigarettes
And a mask of Saagga, the Devil Doctor,
The eyelids worked by strings.

Outside
All around you, there are students researching
With a soft electronic
Hum, but here, where heels clang
On iron grates, voices are at best
Disrespectful: 'Please sir, where's the withered
Hand?' For teachers the thesis is salutary

And simple, a hierarchy of progress culminating
In the Entrance Hall, but children are naturally
Unaware and unimpressed by this.

Encountering
'A jay's feather worn as a charm
In Buckinghamshire, Stone',
We cannot either feel that we have come
Far or in any particular direction.
Item. A dowser's twig, used by Webb
For locating the spring, 'an excellent one',
For Lord Pembroke's waterworks at Dinton
Village. 'The violent twisting is shown
On both limbs of the fork.'

Yes
You have come upon the fabled lands where myths
Go when they die,
But some, especially the Brummagem capitalist
Juju, have arrived prematurely. Idols
Cast there and sold to tribes for a huge
Price for human sacrifice do
(Though slightly hidden) actually exist
And we do well to bring large parties
Of schoolchildren here to find them.

Outdated
Though the cultural anthropological system be
The lonely and unpopular
Might find the landscape of their childhood marked out
Here, in the chaotic piles of souvenirs.
The claw of a condor, the jaw-bone of a dolphin,

These cleave the sky and the waves but they
Would trace from their windowseats the stormy petrel's path
From Lindness or Naze to the North Cape,
Sheltered in the trough of the wave.

James Fenton
(1949–)

Morris Dancers

Deckt out in ribbons gay and papers cut
Fine as a maidens fancy off they strut
And act the morris dance from door to door
Their highest gains a penny nothing more
The children leave their toys to see them play
And laughing maidens lay their work away
The stolen apple in her apron lies
To give her lover in his gay disguise
Een the old woman leaves her knitting off
And lays the bellows in her lap to laugh
Upon the floor the stool made waggons lie
And playing scholars lay the lesson bye
The cat and dog in wonder run away
And hide beneath the table from the fray.

John Clare
(1793–1864)

Stonehenge

from: The Wonders of England

Neere *Wilton* sweete, huge heaps of stones are found,
    But so confused, that neither any eye
    Can count them just, nor reason reason trye,
    What force brought them to so unlikely ground.

Sir Philip Sidney
(1554–1586)

Stonehenge

Observatory, altar, temple, tomb,
Erected none knows when by none knows whom,
To serve strange gods or watch familiar stars,
We drive to see you in our motor cars
And carry picture postcards back to town
While still the unsleeping stars look coldly down.

Sir John Squire
(1884–1958)

The Roman Road

The Roman Road runs straight and bare
As the pale parting-line in hair
Across the heath. And thoughtful men
Contrast its days of Now and Then
And delve, and measure, and compare;

Visioning on the vacant air
Helmed legionaries, who proudly rear
The Eagle, as they pace again
                    The Roman Road.

But no tall brass-helmed legionnaire
Haunts it for me. Uprises there
A mother's form upon my ken,
Guiding my infant steps, as when
We walked that ancient thoroughfare,
                    The Roman Road.

Thomas Hardy
(1840–1928)

The Rolling English Road

Before the Roman came to Rye or out to Severn strode,
The rolling English drunkard made the rolling English road.
A reeling road, a rolling road, that rambles round the shire,
And after him the parson ran, the sexton and the squire;
A merry road, a mazy road, and such as we did tread
The night we went to Birmingham by way of Beachy Head.

I knew no harm of Bonaparte and plenty of the Squire,
And for to fight the Frenchman I did not much desire;
But I did bash their baggonets because they came arrayed
To straighten out the crooked road an English drunkard made,
Where you and I went down the lane with ale-mugs in our hands,
The night we went to Glastonbury by way of Goodwin Sands.

His sins they were forgiven him; or why do flowers run
Behind him; and the hedges all strengthening in the sun?
The wild thing went from left to right and knew not which was
which,
But the wild rose was above him when they found him in the ditch.
God pardon us, nor harden us; we did not see so clear
The night we went to Bannockburn by way of Brighton Pier.

My friends, we will not go again or ape an ancient rage,
Or stretch the folly of our youth to be the shame of age,
But walk with clearer eyes and ears this path that wandereth,
And see undrugged in evening light the decent inn of death;
For there is good news yet to hear and fine things to be seen,
Before we go to Paradise by way of Kensal Green.

G. K. Chesterton

(1874–1936)

Arrivals, Departures

The Lilac is in Bloom

from: The Old Vicarage, Grantchester
(Café des Westens, Berlin, May 1912)

Just now the lilac is in bloom,
All before my little room;
And in my flower-beds, I think,
Smile the carnations and the pink;
And down the borders, well I know,
The poppy and the pansy blow...
Oh! there the chestnuts, summer through,
Beside the river make for you
A tunnel of green gloom, and sleep
Deeply above; and green and deep
The stream mysteriously glides beneath,
Green as a dream and deep as death.
 – Oh, damn! I know it! and I know
How the May fields all golden show,
And when the day is young and sweet,
Gild gloriously the bare feet
That run to bathe...

  Ah God! to see the branches stir
Across the moon at Grantchester!
To smell the thrilling-sweet and rotten
Unforgettable, unforgotten
River-smell, and hear the breeze
Sobbing in the little trees.
Say, do the elm-clumps greatly stand
Still guardians of that holy land?
The chestnuts shade, in reverend dream,
The yet unacademic stream?

Is dawn a secret shy and cold
Anadyomene, silver-gold?
And sunset still a golden sea
From Haslingfield to Madingley?
And after, ere the night is born,
Do hares come out about the corn?
Oh, is the water sweet and cool,
Gentle and brown, above the pool?
And laughs the immortal river still
Under the mill, under the mill?
Say, is there Beauty yet to find?
And Certainty? and Quiet kind?
Deep meadows yet, for to forget
The lies, and truths, and pain?... oh! yet
Stands the Church clock at ten to three?
And is there honey still for tea?

Rupert Brooke
(1887–1915)

Home Thoughts from Abroad

I

Oh, to be in England
Now that April's there,
And whoever wakes in England
Sees, some morning, unaware,
That the lowest boughs and brushwood sheaf
Round the elm-tree bole are in tiny leaf,
While the chaffinch sings on the orchard bough
In England – now!

II

And after April, when May follows,
And the whitethroat builds, and all the swallows!
Hark, where my blossomed pear-tree in the hedge
Leans to the field and scatters on the clover
Blossoms and dewdrops – at the bent spray's edge –
That's the wise thrush; he sings each song twice over,
Lest you should think he never could recapture
The first fine careless rapture!
And though the fields look rough with hoary dew
All will be gay when noontide wakes anew
The buttercups, the little children's dower
 – Far brighter than this gaudy melon-flower!

Robert Browning
(1812–1889)

Departure to the Country

from: Don Juan, Canto XIII

The English winter – ending in July,
        To recommence in August – now was done.
'Tis the postilion's paradise: wheels fly;
        On roads, east, south, north, west, there is a run.
But for post-horses who finds sympathy?
        Man's pity for himself, or for his son,
Always premising that said son at college
Has not contracted much more debt than knowledge.

The London winter's ended in July –
        Sometimes a little later. I don't err
In this: whatever other blunders lies
        Upon my shoulders, here I must aver
My Muse a glass of weatherology;
        For Parliament is our barometer:
Let radicals its other acts attack,
Its sessions form our only almanack.

When its quicksilver's down at zero, – lo!
        Coach, chariot, luggage, baggage, equipage!
Wheels whirl from Carlton Place to Soho,
        And happiest they who horses can engage;
The turnpikes glow with dust; and Rotten Row
        Sleeps from the chivalry of this bright age;
And tradesmen, with long bills and longer faces,
Sigh – as the postboys fasten on the traces.

They and their bills, 'Arcadians both', are left
        To the Greek kalends of another session.

Alas! to them of ready cash bereft,
    What hope remains? Of *hope* the full possession,
Or generous draft, conceded as a gift,
    At a long date – till they can get a fresh one –
Hawk'd about at a discount, small or large;
Also the solace of an overcharge.

But these are trifles. Downward flies my lord,
    Nodding beside my lady in his carriage.
Away! away! 'Fresh horses!' are the word,
    And changed as quickly as hearts after marriage;
The obsequious landlord hath the change restored;
    The postboys have no reason to disparage
Their fee; but ere the water'd wheels may hiss hence,
The ostler pleads too for a reminiscence.

'Tis granted; and the valet mounts the dickey
    That gentleman of lords and gentlemen;
Also my lady's gentlewoman, tricky,
    Trick'd out, but modest more than poet's pen
Can paint, – *'Cosi viaggino i Ricchi!'*
    (Excuse a foreign slipslop now and then,
If but to show I've travell'd: and what's travel,
Unless it teaches one to quote and cavil?)

The London winter and the country summer
    Were well nigh over. 'Tis perhaps a pity,
When nature wears the gown that doth become her.
    To lose those best months in a sweaty city,

And wait until the nightingale grows dumber,
    Listening debates not very wise or witty,
Ere patriots their true *country* can remember; –
But there's no shooting (save grouse) till September.

Lord George Gordon Byron
(1788–1824)

England

We have no grass locked up in ice so fast
That cattle cut their faces and at last,
When it is reached, must lie them down and starve,
With bleeding mouths that freeze too hard to move.
We have not that delirious state of cold
That makes men warm and sing when in Death's hold.
We have no roaring floods whose angry shocks
Can kill the fishes dashed against their rocks.
We have no winds that cut down street by street,
As easy as our scythes can cut down wheat.
No mountains here to spew their burning hearts
Into the valleys, on our human parts.
No earthquakes here, that ring church bells afar,
A hundred miles from where those earthquakes are.
We have no cause to set our dreaming eyes,
Like Arabs, on fresh streams in Paradise.
We have no wilds to harbour men that tell
More murders than they can remember well.
No woman here shall wake from her night's rest,
To find a snake is sucking at her breast.
Though I have travelled many and many a mile,
And had a man to clean my boots and smile
With teeth that had less bone in them than gold –
Give me this England now for all my world.

W. H. Davies
(1871–1940)

Far in a Western Brookland

A Shropshire Lad, LII

Far in a western brookland
　　That bred me long ago
The poplars stand and tremble
　　By pools I used to know.

There, in the windless night-time,
　　The wanderer, marvelling why,
Halts on the bridge to hearken
　　How soft the poplars sigh.

He hears: no more remembered
　　In fields where I was known,
Here I lie down in London
　　And turn to rest alone.

There, by the starlit fences,
　　The wanderer halts and hears
My soul that lingers sighing
　　About the glimmering weirs.

A. E. Housman
(1859–1936)

Arrivals, Departures

This town has docks where channel boats come sidling;
Tame water lanes, tall sheds, the traveller sees
(His bag of samples knocking at his knees),
And hears, still under slackened engines gliding,
His advent blurted to the morning shore.

And we, barely recalled from sleep there, sense
Arrivals lowing in a doleful distance –
Horny dilemmas at the gate once more.
Come and choose wrong, they cry, *come and choose wrong;*
And so we rise. At night again they sound,

Calling the traveller now, the outward bound:
O not for long, they cry, *not for long –*
And we are nudged from comfort, never knowing
How safely we may disregard their blowing,
Or if, this night, happiness too is going.

Philip Larkin
(1922–1985)

Home from Abroad

Far-fetched with tales of other worlds and ways,
My skin well-oiled with wines of the Levant,
I set my face into a filial smile
To greet the pale, domestic kiss of Kent.

But shall I never learn? That gawky girl,
Recalled so primly in my foreign thoughts,
Becomes again the green-haired queen of love
Whose wanton form dilates as it delights.

Her rolling tidal landscape floods the eye
And drowns Chianti in a dusky stream;
The flower-flecked grasses swim with simple horses,
The hedges choke with roses fat as cream.

So do I breathe the hayblown airs of home,
And watch the sea-green elms drip birds and shadows,
And as the twilight nets the plunging sun
My heart's keel slides to rest among the meadows.

Laurie Lee
(1914–1997)

I Travelled Among Unknown Men

I travelled among unknown men,
   In lands beyond the sea;
Nor England! did I know till then
   What love I bore to thee.

'Tis past, that melancholy dream!
   Nor will I quit thy shore
A second time; for still I seem
   To love thee more and more.

Among thy mountains did I feel
   The joy of my desire;
And she I cherished turned her wheel
   Beside an English fire.

Thy mornings shewed, thy nights concealed
   The bowers where Lucy played;
And thine is, too, the last green field
   Which Lucy's eyes surveyed.

William Wordsworth
(1770–1850)

Index to Poets

Acknowledgements

Hilaire Belloc, 'The Garden Party' from *Complete Verse,* Pimlico (1991). Reproduced with the kind permission of Peters Fraser Dunlop.

John Betjeman, 'Harvest Hymn' and 'Hunter Trials' from *Collected Poems,* John Murray (1979). Reproduced with the kind permission of John Murray Publishers.

Frances Cornford, 'Cambridgeshire' and 'Summer Beach' from *Collected Poems,* Cresset Press (1954). Reproduced with the kind permission of the estate of Frances Cornford.

H.D, 'Street by Street' from 'Cities' from *Collected Poems 1912–1944,* Carcanet Press (1984). Reproduced with the kind permission of Carcanet Press.

Roald Dahl, 'A Hand in the Bird' from *Rhyme Stew,* Puffin (2008). Reproduced with the kind permission of David Higham Associates.

U.A Fanthorpe, 'A Major Road for Romney Marsh' from *Safe as Houses; New and Collected Poems,* Enitharmon Press (2010). Reproduced with the kind permission of the estate of U.A Fanthorpe.

Eleanor and Herbert Farjeon, 'Henry VIII' from *Kings and Queens,* Jane Nissen Books (2002). Reproduced with the kind permission of David Higham Associates.

James Fenton, 'The Museum' from 'The Pitt-Rivers Museum, Oxford' from *Yellow Tulips: Poems 1968–2011,* Faber & Faber (2012). Reproduced with the kind permission of Faber & Faber.

Robert Graves, 'The Country Mansion' from *Robert Graves: Selected by Himself,* Penguin (1961). Reproduced with the kind permission of Carcanet Press.

Ted Hughes, 'Harvest Moon' from *New Selected Poems 1957–1994,* Faber & Faber (1995). Reproduced with the kind permission of Faber & Faber.

Elizabeth Jennings, 'English Wild Flowers' from *The Collected Poems of Elizabeth Jennings,* Carcanet (2012). Reproduced with the kind permission of David Higham Associates.

Philip Larkin, 'Arrivals, Departures' from *Collected Poems,* Faber & Faber (2003). Reproduced with the kind permission of Faber & Faber.

Laurie Lee, 'Home from Abroad' from *Selected Poems,* Andre Deutsch (1983). Reproduced with the kind permission of Curtis Brown.

Norman Nicholson, 'Wall' from *Collected Poems,* Faber & Faber (1994). Reproduced with the kind permission of David Higham Associates.

Alfred Noyes, 'George and the Dragon' from *Collected Poems in One Volume,* John Murray (1950). Reproduced with the kind permission of the Society of Authors.

Sylvia Plath, 'Blackberrying' from *Collected Poems,* Faber & Faber (1981). Reproduced with the kind permission of Faber & Faber.

Alan Ross, 'Test Match at Lords' from *To Whom it May Concern: Poems 1952–1957,* Hamish Hamilton (1958). Reproduced with the kind permission of Curtis Brown.

Vita Sackville-West, 'The Weald of Kent' from *The Land*, Heinemann (1955). Reproduced with the kind permission of Curtis Brown.

Vernon Scannell, 'A Day on the River' from *Collected Poems 1950–1993*, Robson Books (1993). Reproduced with the kind permission of the estate of Vernon Scannell.

Sir John Squire, 'Stonehenge' from *Collected Poems, Macmillan* (1959). Reproduced with the kind permission of Roger Squire.

Picture Credits

Science and Society Picture Library/ NRM/ Pictorial Collection: front cover, 4, 8, 13, 31, 33, 43, 48, 53, 54, 58–59, 65, 74–75, 79, 86, 90, 97, 105, 110, 116, 120–121, 128, 138, 154–155,158.

TfL/ London Transport Museum: 22, 26, 40, 70, 84, 113, 126, 134–135, 142, 144, 151, 163, 170–171.

Editor's Acknowledgements

I would like to thank Lucy Smith and Tina Persaud at Batsford and, as always, my agent Teresa Chris.

Much of my research was done at the Saison Poetry Library at the Royal Festival Hall. Set in the heart of London, overlooking the Thames, this library has an amazing collection of books, fantastic resources online, wonderfully helpful staff and is a joy to use.

Many people helped me with suggestions of poems, in particular, thanks to Louy Piachaud for imparting some order to my initial huge list of possible pieces. As always, most thanks to David Gibb, without whom these anthologies would not be nearly so much fun to compile.